HOW TO RELAX

RELAX

SCIENTIFIC BODY CONTROL

BY

WILLIAM H. "LITTLE BILL" MILLER

NEW YORK

SMITH & DURRELL

PREFACE

DURING A LIFETIME devoted to athletics as a player, coach and student, I had often wondered just what quality the truly great athletes possess to give them such marked superiority over their competitors.

For the answer to this question which puzzles every boy who aspires to stardom, as well as every golfer who tries to chip into the 70's, I went first to the zoo for a study of the animals. Certainly nature has endowed them with the qualities they need. Relaxation, balance, agility, are necessarily instinctive to them.

I used to watch every movement of the snake, the tiger, the antelope, and especially the monkey. By studying them when they were at ease and when they were in action, I noted the manner of their breathing, the speed of their reflex actions, their complete flexibility and their dynamic energy. Here was something that nature used as a key to a source of great power, and I stored these observations away for further thought.

Next I turned to outstanding athletes I had known—"super-athletes," the sports writers call them: Jim Thorpe, Red Grange and Dutch Clark of football fame; Honus Wagner, Babe Ruth, Joe DiMaggio and Carl Hubbell in baseball; Nat Holman and Hank Luisetti, noted for their basketball skill; famous golfers—Bobby Jones, Sam Snead and Lawson Little; tennis stars Bill Tilden and Don Budge; and Joe Louis of boxing renown.

All of these famous athletes seemed to have the power to use some sort of natural law—akin to the ebb and flow of the ocean tide.

To further test my theories, I sought other outstanding athletes. I had the pleasure to be associated with Joe Platak, world's handball champion, in a school of skills. I studied Bobby Riggs, national tennis singles champion, during an entire week of play in the Southern Pacific Championships at Los Angeles. I made special trips to Santa Monica to watch Ned Day, great bowler, in action.

This investigation was not confined to sports. The fencers, the dancers, the singers, all proved sources of invaluable information. While in Hollywood·I studied Sonja Henie while she was skating, and the dancers Fred Astaire and Ray Bolger.

Gradually, a definite pattern began to take shape.

I then tried to bring my theories down to earth. I worked with boys in Oklahoma and with boys' groups in Minnesota, California and Canada; with young men in Y.M.C.A.'s, and in schools and clubs. Following successful courses I had given their sons, several pleased parents asked me to take over the instruction of their daughters. Finally adult men and women came to me to teach them the principles of relaxation I had worked out.

Over a five-year period, I have taught more than seven thousand individuals, both singly and in groups, ranging in age from five to sixty-five years.

My system has become widely known as the "Miller Method." This book, covering the Method, is in response to innumerable requests.

WILLIAM MILLER

Tulsa, Oklahoma
April, 1944

CONTENTS

HOW TO RELAX

~~~~~

CHAPTER I

PHYSICAL RELAXATION

AT NO PERIOD in the world's history was there so great a need for relaxation. Tension saps vitality; and during these strenuous times tension is doubled, in many cases trebled. Only through proper relaxation can the energies be conserved that they may be expended with the utmost efficiency.

Just what is that elusive quality called "relaxation"? To relax means "to loosen," to so limber the muscular system that no tenseness or strain remains. That is its accepted meaning, but literally it means to *re*lax, "to loosen *again*," to acquire once more the ease and freedom of motion that is man's heritage no less than that of the lower animals.

Great athletes possess, in marked degree, this grace of fluidity of movement. Seen in slow motion they are "poetry in action." Like the animals, they have learned how to conserve their energies for that exact moment when they need a burst of power or speed. The same grace and beauty of movement are seen in dancers, singers, and others who achieve outstanding success.

A study of the relaxed poise and harmonious motion of these artists and athletes reveals their secret. They have learned so thoroughly the first essential of relaxation, the "body-flow" resulting from muscular ease and rhythm, that it has become an unconscious part of them. All of them possess the same fundamental principles. In addition to complete mental relaxation, they display three striking physical characteristics:

1. The entire muscular structure is flowing and free from tension.

2. The breathing is from the lower lungs, reaching to the diaphragm, rather than solely from the chest.

3. The lower half of the body—hips, knees, calves, ankles—is completely relaxed.

There have been many opinions as to the medium through which one acquires this invaluable asset, the ability to relax. Some claim that it is purely physical; others contend that as the mind controls the body it must be mental; while others insist that it is psychological, induced through emotional control.

All three, physical, mental and psychological, are intricately involved in complete relaxation. But fundamentally, and *predominantly,* it is physical.

Hence the first requirement is the "unlocking" of the body, the loosening up of the muscular system that, because of constraint acquired through the years, is not working at its full efficiency. As the delicate instruments that direct an airplane can control it only when each part of the plane is in perfect operating order, so must each part of the human structure be thoroughly conditioned before the mind can control it properly.

The bones in the body are fixed and cannot be changed, of course. It is the muscles that need attention, particularly those extending to the wrists, elbows and shoulders, the hips, knees, ankles, and other movable joints. These can be loosened up gradually, restoring the elasticity and flexibility that nature intended they should have. Only when this is accomplished can "unit-flow" of the entire body be achieved. And "unit-flow" is the keynote of relaxation. The complete release of nervous tension and freedom from muscular tightness can result only through complete body-flow.

The golfer knows how essential it is to "follow-through," to secure both power and accuracy in executing a drive. In order to get this complete "follow-through" the entire body from head to foot must be free of muscular tension. If any part —the shoulder, the hip, the knee, the ankle—is stiff, or "locked," a perfect "follow-through" is impossible.

Waite Hoyt, former New York Yankee star pitcher, stated aptly that the objective was to attain "the direct continuity of the body-weight toward a given target."

This continuity of body-weight is the essential body-flow of the muscles—without which there can be no real relaxation.

Physicians prescribe relaxing. Coaches instruct their athletes to practice it. Aviation instructors stress this quality to students as the first essential of flying a plane. And no less is relaxing impera-tive for men and women in war industries, where they are working in unnatural environment and under nerve-straining conditions of noise and speed; for the housewife who is "carrying on" under innumerable adverse conditions; for the busy executive, and for his office staff; and for those many others who through proper relaxation will acquire new verve for the tasks that must be done.

Complete physical relaxation is attained, first, through the thorough but gradual loosening up of the intricate system of muscles which extend throughout the entire body; and, second, through correct breath control.

The exercises in the following chapters have accomplished outstanding results for the thousands who have taken either individual or group instruction in the Miller Method. They should be of the same inestimable benefit to anyone who follows them sincerely.

CHAPTER II

BASIC ROUTINES

THE FIRST STEP is the loosening up of the muscular structure. And in that our first attention is given to the movable joints.

The flexibility of the joints depends partly upon the elasticity and firmness of the ligaments—those strong fibrous bands that fasten the bones together and encircle the joints; and upon the condition of the cartilage which covers the ends of the bones, acts as a buffer and reduces friction. It is the lining of the ends of the cartilage and the inside of the ligaments which secretes the fluid that lubricates the joints.

Very largely the flexibility of movable joints depends upon the condition of the muscles which extend to them and are there attached to the ends of the bones. The contraction or shortening of the muscles, on receiving nerve-impulses from the brain, pulls the ends of the bones closer together and thus produces movement.

The amount of the movement depends upon the nature of the joint. A ball-and-socket joint, such as that of the shoulder and hip, permits much greater freedom of action than the hinge-joint of the elbow and knee. The sliding-joint of the ankle is mostly limited to forward-and-backward movement; while the thumb, with its saddle-joint, can be moved freely either forward-and-backward or sideways.

Muscles allowed to grow flabby and weak, or become too stiff, throw too great a strain upon the ligaments, often to their serious injury, besides materially reducing the physical efficiency of the muscles themselves. Hence the first essential is to tone up the entire muscular system. This is best accomplished by gradually loosening up the muscles, releasing their unnatural tenseness or flabbiness, restoring their vitality and fluidity.

An excellent first-exercise for this purpose is the *Three-way Breakdown,* executed in three stages, which are called, for convenience, *A, B* and *C.* It releases tautness in wrists, shoulders, hips, knees and ankles.

Three-way Breakdown

Position:

Stand with the feet comfortably apart, the toes pointed slightly outward, the arms hanging at the sides.

Bend the right elbow until the forearm is parallel to the floor, the fingers extended their full length. Now bring the forearm in front of the body.

Lower the body by bending the knees and drooping the shoulders. (Do *not* bend over from the waist.) With the right forearm held horizontally just below the knees, measure the distance from *instep to instep*. This should equal the distance from *elbow to extended fingertips*, with the forearm precisely parallel to the floor.

Keeping the feet this distance apart, return to erect position, with the arms hanging easily, full-length, at the sides.

Bend the knees slightly until the weight of the body is on the balls of the feet. The heels

should barely touch the floor. (This slight bending of the knees starts the "breaking" process,
the "unlocking" of tight muscles.)

You are now in the correct position to begin
the exercises—standing erect, arms at the sides,
weight on the balls of the feet, knees slightly
bent, toes turned somewhat outward, feet apart
elbow-to-fingertip distance between the insteps.

A. For Wrist Flexibility:

Bend the elbows until the forearms are parallel to the floor, then bring the hands to the front

of the body, barely removed from each other,
the wrists flexed until the palms face inward.

Keeping the forearms parallel to the floor, rotate them until the palms of the hands are facing the body.

Now shake the wrists. Lightly at first, then with increasing vigor. Execute the movement loosely and lazily.

Work for an *up-and-down* movement of the wrists.

This should materially increase their flexibility—a vital factor for achieving maximum power in throwing a ball of any kind, or in the finish of a golf or batting swing, and indispensable for anyone seeking to attain physical relaxation through a toning up of the complete muscular system.

B. To Loosen Shoulder Muscles:

Keeping the head erect, raise the shoulders exaggeratedly, trying to touch the ears with them. This is not ordinarily possible, but by raising the elbows (allowing the forearms to dangle) the shoulders will go much higher.

Keep the knees slightly bent while executing this upward movement of the shoulders. This is important for the correct execution of the next movement.

Allow the head and shoulders to droop downward until the arms are at full length and the forearms are between the bent knees. This is the relaxed position in which a monkey stands when he is at rest.

At the same time let the entire body, including the head, sag loosely or "flop." The torso and legs move as though you were sitting down in a chair.

Never bend over from the waist.

At the lowest point of this movement, the arms should dangle loosely, full-length. But the fingertips should not touch the floor.

Return to erect position.

This sagging exercise is excellent for a thorough loosening of the shoulder muscles. Also, it effects a definite release of tension.

C. To Loosen Hip Muscles, Knees and Ankles:

Lower the torso, by slightly drooping the shoulders and bending the knees, but do not bend at the waist. Hang the hands between the knees at knee-level, wrists bent until the backs of the hands are parallel to the floor.

Without changing the position of the hands or the arms, work slowly downward until the backs of the hands—from the second joints to the tips of the fingers—lie flat on the floor.

This downward progression is done in four *up-and-down movements,* each gradually carrying the hands lower. The muscles leading to the hips, knees and ankles are thus loosened by degrees, avoiding strain. Allow the weight of the torso and hips to aid in working downward.

Keep the feet stationary. Do not permit the toes to work outward—a common tendency when the knees are stiff, or "locked." However, in each up-and-down movement used in working downward, the ankles, too, should be worked up and down.

(When the knees are unusually tight—as is often the case in middle-age—before attempting this exercise they should be lightly loosened by the *Rhumba Movements.* (These are explained in Chapter IV.)

The return to an erect position is made in three stages.

. 1. Raise the body until the backs of the hands are again at knee-level.

2. Straighten the back, allowing the arms to return to the sides.

3. Return the head to a vertical position.

Neck Exercise

An important step in loosening the muscular system is to take the tension out of the neck. This is done by revolving the head.

Standing in the position described for the *Three-way Breakdown*—the insteps elbow-to-fingertip distance apart, knees slightly flexed—

bend the head well forward in front of the left shoulder.　Look down at the left toe.

Keeping the head well forward, move it over until it is in front of the right shoulder.

Now swing the head slowly backward until it is, as nearly as possible, to the rear of the right shoulder.

Keeping the head *well back,* bring it over to the rear of the left shoulder.

Swing it slowly to the front of the left shoulder.

Then return it to the normal vertical position.

Reverse the exercise by beginning in front of the right shoulder and revolving the head counterclockwise.

It is vital that you do not cut the movement short at any point, *especially in its rearward course.*

This exercise may cause slight dizziness at first. Relieve this by taking a long deep breath up into the chest and then letting the air down into the lower lungs. Simultaneously raise and lower the chest muscles.

FINGERS AND TOES

The constant use of the hands keeps the finger-joints pliable, and the muscles of the feet are exercised by the mere act of walking, for no step is taken without bending the toes. But these joints can be made considerably more limber; and their loosening aids in the general body-flow of all the muscles.

In the Miller Method it is not necessary to lay particular stress upon the joints of the fingers and toes, as they get sufficient loosening exercise during the execution of the other movements.

CHAPTER III

~~~~~~

BREATH CONTROL

ONLY AFTER THE muscular system has been taught
to "let go" completely can proper breath control
be achieved. This is the second phase of the process
of relaxing through the co-ordination of natural
breathing and natural movement.

Correct breath control is acquired only when
the system has been trained to utilize the maximum capacity of the lungs, when the breathing
is deep, filling the lower part of the lungs, with
the consequent full exercise of the diaphragm.

The diaphragm, it will be recalled, is that thin,
strong, arched muscular partition which separates
the chest cavity—containing the heart and the
lungs—from the abdominal cavity. It plays a vital
part in respiration, through its ability to contract,
with the intake of a deep breath, until it is almost

16

straight, thereby enlarging the chest cavity.

The mechanism of breathing, intricate in all its details, can nevertheless be stated simply. Many muscles besides the diaphragm are brought into play. The nerve-cells that control them are grouped at the base of the brain, at the "breathing-center." Carbon dioxide in the blood stimulates these cells, causing them to send, at regular intervals, nerve-impulses to all the muscles involved. The muscles respond by contracting and air fills the lungs, bringing oxygen to the blood to replace its over-accumulation of carbon dioxide. The expiration of the breath carries off this unwanted carbon dioxide, and as the air leaves the lungs the contracted muscles relax—until they receive the next nerve-impulse from the brain.

As a full breath, laden with oxygen, is brought into the lungs, their elasticity enables them to expand; and simultaneously the chest cavity enlarges to allow them plenty of room for the expansion. This is accomplished in three ways: The breastbone, regulated by important muscles, moves upward and forward as the muscles contract. The ribs lift and move outward. The diaphragm, the muscular floor of the cavity, is pushed downward by its contraction. During expiration the movements are reversed.

This explains not only the necessity for proper, full breathing, to expand the lungs and thus the chest cavity, but the need for co-ordinating the intake and outgo of breath with the rhythmic flow of the chest muscles. Only so can "natural" breathing be achieved.

The following exercise should accomplish this.

THREE-WAY BREATH CONTROL

A. Loosening Chest Muscles:

Stand erect with the feet apart—the elbow-to-fingertip distance.

Keep the knees *straight* and draw the stomach well in.

Now bend over *from the waist* and try to place the backs of the forearms together—from elbow to wrist. This is virtually impossible for most people, but even the attempt will accomplish the desired purpose, which is to pull the shoulders as far forward as possible.

Turn the head from side to side and try to touch each shoulder with the chin.

Lean still farther forward from the waist.

Keep the stomach *held well in* while doing this.

Touch the farthest possible point on the shins with extended fingertips—the arms full-length.

While this is being done very slowly, say slowly, *"Take—it—o-u-t!"*—meaning to pull the breath out of the diaphragm. End the words with the finish of the downward movement.

B. *Controlling the Breath:*

Slowly straighten up again, pulling the breath high into the upper chest.

At the same time, slowly bring the shoulders well back—*not high,* however, as this creates tension.

While the body is slowly straightening up, slide the fingertips slowly up the shins and over the knees. At this point—the knees—the web between the first finger and the thumb comes into use.

Allow this web to straddle the thigh, sliding

up it until, with the shoulders at the rearmost point, the webs are stationed opposite the crotch of the legs.

While executing this upward movement, say slowly, *"Take—it—u-p!"*—meaning to draw the breath high up into the chest.

C: Relaxing Exercise:

Slowly and gradually permit the entire body to slump. Completely *relax the muscles*. At the same time let the breath slowly down again into the lower lungs.

Slump downward until the entire weight of the upper part of the body is resting on the *straightened arms*.

The web between the first finger and the

thumb slides slowly down the front of the thigh during this slump, until it rests *against* and *above* the knee cap.

Simultaneously, while *slowly* executing this downward movement, say the word, *"S-a-g!"*

At the lowest point of the slump, swing the chin from side to side, attempting to touch each shoulder.

This entire relaxing movement is tremendously important. When it is properly done, three things take place simultaneously:

1. The air is let out between slightly parted lips and drops naturally into the lower lungs.

2. The outward and forward bend of the knees begins with the *first outgo of breath* between the lips.

3. The shoulders commence their forward movement.

Slowly straighten the body until you are again standing at ease in a normal position, the hands at the sides.

TOTAL RELAXATION

The body is *completely relaxed* when the joints —wrists, elbows, shoulders, hips, knees, ankles—

are all flexed or bent and the entire muscular system is loose or gone slack; and the breath is deep in the lower lungs.

The complete co-ordination of breathing and movement is the secret of body-flow and relaxation. As you execute the following exercise, imagine that the muscles and the breath are "teammates."

Co-ordinating Breathing and Movement:

At the lowest point of the *C* stage, the relaxing exercise, of the *Three-way Breath Control* given above, remove the hands from above the kneecaps and turn them over between the knees, with the palms upward. Spread the fingers comfortably apart and hold them relaxed—taut fingers evidence strain.

Now slowly raise the arms and lengthen the entire body until the arms are full-length overhead.

As you do this with a *long stretching movement* of the entire muscular system, draw the breath up high into the chest.

Keeping this position, rise on the toes.

Come slowly downward again to a slumped position. Literally let the body fold like an accordion.

At the lowest point once more, the knees and the elbows should be well bent. Return the elbows, keeping them flexed, to the sides.

The breath has been dropped deep into the diaphragm.

All muscles should be utterly loose. Let yourself go!

This complete "letting go" of the muscular system and the breathing is called "Pressing the Button." When this has been mastered, you can *relax at will.*

Follow the Basic Routines (in preceding chapter) and Breath Control with a hot bath, which intensifies the relaxing effect. Finish with a dash of cold water to close the pores and prevent possibly catching cold.

~~~~~

CHAPTER IV

RHYTHM IN MOVEMENT

To THE ANCIENT Greeks, whose sculptures are such exquisite studies in rhythm, this word meant "flow," or "measured flow"; and that is its meaning today, a harmonious and regular recurrence of motion or sound. The ancients recognized three kinds of rhythm: that of tones—music; that of words—poetry; and that of bodily movement and attitudes.

In the human body the flow of the involuntary muscles is a beautiful balance of poise and rhythm. The beat of the heart, its contraction, its pause, its relaxing, is rhythmic; the measured expansion and contraction of the chest in breathing is rhythmic. There is response to rhythmic sound, such as the tick of a clock, the steady drip of water.

It is the muscles under our control which must

be so relaxed and conditioned that they will flow
in harmony with the body's involuntary rhythm.
It is impossible for us to produce rhythmic actions
deliberately. Only when a movement is repeated
until it is performed with no conscious thought,

no deliberate effort, is there natural rhythm. This
is seen in the measured steps of marching, in running, in dancing, in the swing of the woodman's
ax.

The rhythmic harmony of the muscular system
—in other words, perfect body-flow—permits
freer circulation of the blood, which in turn tones
up the entire system. And in the graceful movements resulting from rhythmic balance, there is a
saving of energy, and consequently less fatigue
and greater endurance.

Outstanding athletes, the most talented dancers,
singers, skaters, display natural rhythm in all their
movements. Forced or jerky motions mark the
mediocre performer. The baseball player and the

boxer can borrow from the theater. Some forward-looking trainers of athletes already have sensed the usefulness of rhythm in their work.

Knute Rockne, Notre Dame's immortal coach, sat in a theater marveling at the precision and rhythm of a line of dancing girls. He thought: "What complete harmony! What co-ordination!" Could this be applied to football?

Returning to the practice field, he experimented with the idea with his backfield men. He taught them to move in unison, in a co-ordinated "shift." The results were gratifying. The marvelous co-ordination shown by the famed "Four Horse-men" and later Notre Dame backfields is largely credited to this idea.

A few years prior to World War II Mussolini engaged Boyd Comstock, the University of Southern California's well-known track coach, to work with Italian athletes. The object was to improve their performances at the Olympic Games. Comstock worked tirelessly at the task. But it seemed almost hopeless, until the canny American trainer hit on an idea.

He had observed that these Italian youths were passionately fond of music. Could the natural rhythm they showed in singing, for instance, be applied also to track? At least it was worth a trial. So Comstock told his protégés to sing as they ran, hurdled and jumped. Almost miraculous improvements resulted, Comstock reported.

Early in my own experimental work I made a discovery that illustrates the value of rhythm. My attempts to teach a girl to play tennis were going slowly. Her technique was all right. She held her racket correctly, her stance was good and she pivoted properly as she tried to stroke the ball. But all her movements were studied, mechanical. In sheer desperation I turned to music.

"Mary, do you know the words to the *Blue Danube Waltz?*" I asked.

"Why, yes, Mr. Miller," the girl replied in astonishment.

"I'm probably the world's worst when it comes to music—but let's try singing it in time to the movements."

Here's the way it went: *"Merrily o'er each tiny*

wave (rhythmically she took a long breath and raised her arm, then brought it down to position) *"now dances our bark o'er coral cave"* (she moved backward and her racket came forward again in a long sweep). The result was perfect. The girl had hit the ball in a perfect drive.

Often, when coaching basketball, I have been struck by the similarity in bodily movements between the dancer and the man aiming for the basket. For example, a player "takes off" in the air as he nears the goal to shoot. His knees bend lithely. His body turns gracefully in the air as he positions his hands for the shot. Study the pictures of the formal Egyptian dancer. Note the similarity in pose.

Certain simple steps of the rhumba have proved of value in teaching rhythm in connection with relaxation and body-flow.

They also have another purpose. There is one vital area which the "unlocking" exercises given in the preceding chapters fail to reach completely. The muscles surrounding the base of the spine must be kept loose to aid in keeping the spine flexible. (A flexible spine is essential to good health.) There is nothing finer for this purpose than these two rhumba exercises:

RHUMBA MOVEMENTS

A. Foot movement.

Place the feet almost together, the toes pointing directly forward. The arms should hang
loosely at the sides.

Adjust the entire body to complete relaxation
with long upward and downward movements
of muscles and breath.

Then "break," or slightly flex, the knees,
placing the weight on the balls of the feet.

Take a fairly long sideways step to the left
and rest the weight on the left side. Keep the
left knee very slightly bent.

Draw the right foot, *on the toe,* over to the
left instep.

Keeping the weight centered on the left side, play the right foot lightly out and in.

This movement is done to a 1-2-3 count. On *1*, take a long step left and draw the other foot over. On *2*, play the foot out. On *3*, play it in again.

Alternate the movement. Take a long step with the right foot and play the left foot out and in *on the toe*.

B. Knee Movement.

Duplicate the above movements, but instead of letting the "playing foot" go out and in, *keep the toe stationary,* and simply allow the knee *to waggle exaggeratedly out and in.*

This movement, especially, cultivates complete flexibility in the ankle, knee and hip.

In the true rhumba movement, the upper half of the body is held stationary—*but not stiff*—while the lower half works with complete looseness.

~~~~~~~~

CHAPTER V

BODY BALANCE

BODY BALANCE MIGHT be defined as the mainte-
nance of the various parts of the body in their
correct positions in relation to each other, whether
at rest or in action, to counteract the natural pull
of gravity.

An off-balance posture upsets the muscle and
ligament mechanism by causing undue shortening
and tightening on one side and stretching and
weakening on the other. Thus a body out of natural alignment experiences fatigue more quickly
and has much less endurance than the one with
perfect balance.

All outstanding athletes display body balance;
it is the very foundation of their play. To them
correct balance means the ability to start instantly
in any given direction, to shift weight smoothly,

and to be perfectly poised at all times, no matter in what position they may find themselves.

A cardinal principle of good body balance is that the arms and legs must be properly flexed. Try this experiment. Hold the hand out at arm's-length, and see how fast a move can be made with the arm in that position. Now bend the arm fully at the elbow. Note how much quicker a movement can be made.

The athlete knows that the speed of the striking movement comes from the bent elbow; and that to move with instantaneous speed in any direction, the legs must be bent at the knees. Like the quick-starting animals—the cat, the tiger, the leopard— you must crouch for a fast start. And crouching means well-bent knees.

The following five-step exercise, helpful in developing perfect balance, has been used by me both in teamwork and in individual instruction for many years, and always with splendid results. While its basic object is to train the body to move with cat-like quickness, it materially aids in the complete muscle-flow which is essential to body balance.

FIVE-STEP BALANCE METHOD

1. Measure:

Measure the distance between the feet, following the directions given at the beginning of the *Three-way Breakdown* exercise in Chapter II. The distance between the insteps should equal that from the elbow to the extended fingertips.

In the present exercise, however, the right foot is stationed a little farther back than the left, with the toe of the right foot opposite the left instep.

It is important that the toes point slightly outward. If the feet are pointed directly forward, when the knees are bent properly outward the weight will be thrown on the extreme outside of the foot, and not, as it should be, squarely on the ball of the foot. On the other hand, if the toes point outward too much, you are thrown into an equally awkward position.

2. Sag:

Raise the breath slowly high into the chest, simultaneously drawing up the muscles until the thumb-web straddles the *front* of the thigh opposite the crotch of the legs.

Now let the body completely slump, precisely as explained in the *C* movement of the *Three-way Breath Control* in Chapter III.

As the body slumps downward the knees should bend *squarely over and onto the balls of the feet.*

3. *Ready:*

Lean still farther onto the ball of the right foot. *Do not throw the weight on the side of the foot*—a common fault.

Raise the left arm, elbow bent, to about shoulder-level. Open the fingers, literally "feeling the air."

Instructing the Cincinnati Reds on how to relax.

Tulsa University backfield "unlocking" prior to a game, with Coach Henry Frnka looking on.

The position of the right arm is at full-length, well to the rear of the right side.

Now every ounce of weight is concentrated in the opposite direction from that in which the move is to be made—a cardinal principle in body-flow.

Mentally liken your body to that of an airplane, your arms to the wings. If a wing were folded to the body of a plane, the ship would lose balance and crash. Just so with your body. The arms should be fully used in maintaining good balance. An object held in one hand—football, tennis racket—should always be counterbalanced by extending the opposite arm.

4. Pivot:

Before beginning the pivoting movement, swing the right arm gently to and fro, allowing the body to sway gently with the movement.

Keep the entire body *loose and relaxed*.

Pivot to the left, making at least a three-quarter turn, using the ball of the left foot as the pivoting-point.

There are two vital points about executing a perfect pivot. First, *do not come up in the slightest degree* in making the turn. Second, *do not bring the feet together*. (At the halfway point, however, the right foot will swing in close to the left heel and then at the close swing out again.) At the close of the pivot the relative position of the feet and the distance between them should be the same as at the beginning of the movement.

At the finish of the pivot, bring the right arm up in front of your chest, the elbow bent. Both arms will then be in identical positions.

5. *Shift:*

With the weight on the balls of the feet, hands upraised in front of you, shift from side to side.

The shifting is done by pulling the right foot in to the left, then pushing the left foot out until the original distance is attained. Done swiftly, it is *one continuous motion*. It is a *glide,* not a jump.

As a practical reminder for the above *Five-step Balance Method,* with the first finger of the right hand tap out the order of the movements on the fingers of the left hand, saying them aloud as you do so:

"Measure"—little finger.
"Sag"—third finger.
"Ready'—second finger.
"Pivot"—first finger.
"Shift"—thumb.

BODY-FLOW DRILLS

The chief purpose of these drills is to perfect body balance through the proper and easy flow of the muscles.

A. Skating Drill:
Take the *Ready* position in the *Five-step Balance Method* described above. Come loosely and lazily to this position.

Move the body diagonally to the left and forward by shifting the feet in a panther-like glide.

Pause.

The left knee should now be bent well over the left foot. The head and eyes are centered directly over the left knee.

Now remove the weight from the ball of the left foot, which has been solidly planted, in a diagonal shift to the right and forward with the right foot.

This drill is exactly as though you were skating.

As the move is made, for instance to the left, the right foot follows and comes to a point near the left heel.

Then a pivot is made on the ball of the right foot, and at the right shift the left foot trails the other.

B. *Long Body-flow:*

This long body-flow drill is excellent for inducing unit-flow.

Stand with the feet elbow-to-fingertip distance apart.

Hold a heavy object—a book, hammer, anything convenient—in both hands at waist-level.

Raise the object—a book, let us say—high over the head in front, simultaneously drawing breath up into the upper chest.

Then *completely relax,* lowering the book and dropping the breath into the diaphragm.

With *no conscious effort,* hold the book high to the left in the *right hand only.* As this is done, the left foot should turn on the ball of the foot, the knees slightly bent.

Now, let the weight of the book swing your shoulders down and up again with the book

held high to the right. The right foot will turn naturally on the ball of the foot.

The head should always turn to follow the movement.

In the downward swing, the knees should be well bent and the book almost graze the floor.

All parts of the body should be utterly loose and flow freely in this long swing.

Executed properly, there should be such a complete flow of weight that the toe of the rear foot is dragged somewhat. *Let yourself go completely!*

(Incidentally, this is an excellent drill for the improvement of one's golf swing.)

C. Dual Drill:

Two persons face each other at three-quarter level.

The weight is on the balls of the feet, the hands held at chest-level almost against the body, with the elbows well bent.

The palms, turned outward, and the fingers form twin vertical walls.

It is wise to come to this stance after first doing the *Sag* movement of the *Five-step Balance Method*. This insures relaxation, which is important to this drill.

Extending your left arm, and allowing the shoulder to follow freely, and the left knee to bend, strike your partner's right hand (held stationary) with your left hand. Then alternate by extending your right arm, and *bending the right knee,* and striking his left hand *lightly* with your right hand.

Work slowly at first, then at a faster pace.

Your partner should step backward, while you continue the alternate thrust of arm and shoulder.

Then it is your partner's turn. He does the striking with alternate hands, while you become the target, your hands held stationary, palms outward, in front of your chest.

It will be found that if the knees do not work in and out concurrently with the striking motion, balance will be lost and the body will topple forward.

Correctly executed, the drill will develop the ability to employ both sides of the body almost equally well.

D. *Spinning-top Test:*

Take the *Ready* position of the *Five-step Balance Method.*

Stay "loose as a goose."

Swinging the right arm, spiral round and round over the floor, using the balls of the feet as pivot-points.

Following the initial swing of the arm, the feet will come almost together.

Practice until you can spin fifteen to twenty times without losing balance.

These fundamental routines and movements should be practiced over and over. Then and then only will you have good balance under all conditions. The man who must stop to think of the right or forceful word is not a good speaker. Similarly, relaxation and body-flow must become so natural that they seem to be a part of yourself.

~~~

CHAPTER VI

BODY CONTROL

POSSIBLY THE MOST important thing in the science of body control-is the proper distribution of weight.

Glance down at your feet as you walk. Do the toes point outward as you take that forward stride? If so, the weight is being thrown off-center, to the inside of the feet. To this severe strain of muscles and ligaments is added constriction of the blood-flow to the pedal extremities.

What causes the feet to turn outward?

In many cases it is because the child was meticulously taught to walk so, being constantly reminded to turn his toes out, until he had acquired a lifelong habit.

But the most common cause of this faulty dis-

tribution of body-weight is "knee-lock." The
muscles leading to the knees are stiff from disuse,
or excess fat is present. The knees once permitted
to stiffen will not bend easily without effort. So
their owner avoids bending the knees by turning
the feet outward as he walks.

Observe the long, comfortable stride of the
woodsman or the Indian. His feet are placed
directly forward with each step. The toes point,
if anything, slightly inward as he walks. In order
to achieve this easy forward method of locomo-
tion, the rear knee must bend so that the weight
falls directly upon the ball of the foot as each
step is taken.

There is a simple natural law covering the correct distribution of weight. The weight of the
leg in all movements should be squarely into and
over the ball of the foot. The latter is a natural
base designed for that express purpose.

The Knee:

Why should faulty knee action be so common among men, women and children? It is largely because of methods of early physical training. We are either thrown out to run around like long-legged colts, stiff-legged, or are given types of formal calisthenics which stress keeping the knees straight. This leads to "jamming the joints." The knees are not given the constant bending necessary to retain flexibility and elasticity.

This is shown most forcibly in the simple act of picking up objects. The ball player misses a ground ball, the housewife develops an aching back, the elderly man wrenches a muscle or tendon. All for the same simple fundamental reason. They are not using the knees in the way that nature intended, to lower the body. They are bending from the waist.

A new recruit joined the Cincinnati Reds in the spring for training. I watched him carefully. Then, strolling casually over, I offered a question.

"When you are not playing baseball what do you work at?"

"Coal mining," he replied, a trifle puzzled.

"How would you pick up a hundred-pound lump of coal? Show me."

He obligingly complied, using a squatting movement which employed well-bent knees.

"Why didn't you just bend over from the waist?" I asked.

"Oh, you never pick up a lump of coal with your arms," he exclaimed.

"Why not?"

"You'd hurt your back. You have to let the leg and thigh muscles take the load."

"Right! And every time you field a grounder I want you to pretend that you're picking up a big lump of coal. Sit down to the ball. Never bend over from the waist."

This same rule holds true for the housewife. Never bend from the waist in picking up an object. A simple way to remember this is to avoid

reaching out in front of you. Place yourself directly beside the object before you stoop. This will force you to bend your knees, thus keeping the joints flexible.

The Hand:

The human body is a marvelous machine. More intricate than the most complicated scientific instrument, it is yet amazingly simple in its workings. Each of its many parts is designed for a specific use.

Consider the hand, for example. Doubled into a fist, it can be made as hard as iron, striking with crushing force. But the next instant this same hand can be made pliable and stroke with velvet touch; it can handle the most delicate material without injury, or strike the keys of a piano or the strings of a violin with incredible rapidity.

But despite our constant use of the hand and our familiarity with it, few of us utilize its complete range of efficiencies.

Take, as an example, the field of sports. The athlete has at his command a web, the connecting tissue between his fingers, enabling him to widen or narrow the distance between them at will. Yet how rarely does he use this to the fullest advantage!

For instance, maximum hand surface is vital to the sure catching of a football or basketball. Just before he starts to catch a ball the average player runs toward it with his fingers held more or less close together. Only at the actual instant of reception or as he throws up his hands does he start to open his fingers fully.

This is not mere thoughtlessness, nor is it due to lack of knowledge of the most advantageous position of the fingers. It is a lack of the automatic control of the hand muscles which should spread the fingers even in the pitch of excitement. It is obvious that if the player opens his hands— not so widely, however, that he loses instant flexibility—before he catches the ball, the widest possible surface will be applied at the instant it is caught. This maximum surface spells sureness. It can be achieved through muscle control, which must become so instinctive that the hand will respond without conscious thought.

How to Fall:

Falls cause an incredible number of accidents each year, each day even. Next to the importance of prevention, by exercising more care, more common sense, is the value of knowing *how* to fall.

You have to learn the trick of collapsing. This is part of the training in body control.

If, as you start to fall, the knees are bent and the body thus commences a collapsing movement, joint by joint, usually no serious injury will result. Combined with this voluntary looseness of the joints, the entire muscular structure should be *completely relaxed,* with no tautness anywhere.

It will be well to recall the old circus acrobat's sage advice:

"Just sag like an old sock."

CHAPTER VII

MENTAL RELAXATION

COMPLETE PHYSICAL RELAXATION has a direct bearing upon mental relaxation. The looseness and flow of the body, easing the strain upon the nerve-centers of the brain, leaves the mind less fatigued and so capable of clearer and more forceful thinking.

While it is true that without the symmetrical action of the brain there could be no precision and ease of movements, freedom of movements in turn aids in regulating that symmetrical action of the brain.

On countless occasions I have been asked, "Isn't relaxation simply a state of the mind?" Emphatically I answer in the negative. When someone is of a naturally even or genial disposition it will, of course, be revealed in the movements of

Teaching business men to relax.

Leading the Oklahoma University basketball squad in "body balance" drills.

his body. They will be characteristically easy or relaxed.

But with a person of more dynamic nature mental control with respect to inducing relaxation is more difficult. Thought will not "unlock" a tight muscle. It is first necessary to apply in a practical way a patient process for "loosening up" a muscular area. Only when the physical system is conditioned can mental control be fully efficient.

During my coaching experience I had impressed upon me strongly a vital principle of teaching. No one fully retains that which they do not thoroughly understand. Simply teaching physical routines will not "get the job done." Much time must be spent in conveying logical reasons for the things taught.

A young basketball coach came to me on several occasions for advice. The physical steps were demonstrated to him thoroughly. I also explained the methods of application. However, little progress took place. Once more he sought my suggestions. In sheer desperation I made a final recommendation. This was for me to take his squad for a session behind locked doors. He accepted the proposition gratefully.

At the outset I asked the boys, who ranged in age from twelve to fifteen years, to be seated. Carefully I explained the reason for each fundamental of body mechanics behind the execution of basketball maneuvers. Then we went into actual practice. The results obtained in the one two-hour session were almost unbelievable. Before the close these youthful athletes had completed no less than nine "perfect plays." By this term I mean that each maneuver in a particular formation—pivots, passes and shots, etc.—was executed perfectly by each member taking part.

Even at this tender age the value of coupling the mental with the physical was thus forcefully demonstrated. Those going deeply into the subject, invariably state that the potentialities of using the mind in training the body have never been fully explored. Certain experiments that I have made tend to confirm this strongly.

For instance, I found that it was possible to shoot goals with a basketball while blindfolded. This aroused much curiosity. But my procedure was simple.

Immediately before the demonstration I would thoroughly "unlock" the muscular system from head to foot. Then I would go deliberately through the breath-control method. (These are explained in detail in Chapters II and III.) As a bucket was placed over my head I would say silently, "Go to work!" This intensely concentrated command was addressed figuratively to what I thought of as a little man in the "control tower"—or the brain.

In effect, I was consciously pouring the power of the mind back into the body. I found that it was possible in that way to duplicate things that had been done with the eyes open.

Rod Warren, director for Grantland Rice "Sportlight" films, offered an interesting comment at the end of one of these demonstrations. He observed:

"Bill, when you make shots with your eyes closed your whole body seems to smooth out. The movements are fluid as water."

Many business executives after the adoption of relaxation routines have commented upon the beneficial effect of the exercises on their ability to think clearly.

Recently one of these men made an important trip through mid-western cities for his concern. On his return he said, "Every day on returning to my hotel room I went through the relaxation routines. I followed them with a hot bath. I enjoyed every step I took, each bite I ate. But I also believe that I did the finest two-weeks work of my life."

Do the little irritations of life upset you?

Some years ago I was watching a friend working with a typewriter ribbon. Suddenly it slipped out of its tiny holder for the third time. A spool went rolling across the desk. Patiently he retrieved it and tried once more.

"Doesn't that make you angry?" I inquired.

"I never allow myself to become angry over inanimate things," he replied. This wise observation has been of value to me innumerable times since.

What is your customary reaction to the little things which won't seem to go right? To that missed train connection? To the accidental breaking of that lens? To the resignation of that valuable employee? Does it unduly disturb you? Do you allow yourself to say a few strong words, then grudgingly set about correcting the matter?

Each of these things, in itself, is minor. But multiplied they build tension in the system.

The next time you accidentally knock over a pile of papers, for instance, try this. Quietly and calmly, without thought of any possible irritation involved, pick them up. If you will do this whenever you are distressed, you will definitely contribute to your over-all health, your ability to relax both mentally and physically.

Recently a secretary ushered me into an office. Presently, the business man with whom I had an appointment came storming in. He appeared extremely angry. After he had greeted me, he launched into the cause of his anger.

"I tell you," he said, "if conditions continue as they are, I'm going to get a gun and go after some blankety-blank..."

I listened a few minutes more. Then I smiled as disarmingly as possible and said quietly, "So what?"

"So what?" he repeated. "What do you mean?"

"This is just a phase, a trend. These things run in cycles. Conditions may not be to your liking today but the pendulum always swings back. A year or two from now you'll find it hard to remember what all the shouting was about."

"Perhaps you're right," he somewhat grudgingly admitted.

"Yes, this phase will pass. But that isn't important. What is important is that you will have done perhaps irremediable harm to your nerves and well-being."

Schooling oneself to adopt the "so what" attitude is definitely practical in learning to relax the mind. What has happened is a fact accomplished, water over the dam, milk spilled. Nothing is gained by bewailing it. Cultivate the ability to turn quietly and coolly to that which is to be done.

CHAPTER VIII

LADIES, RELAX!

THERE ARE MANY problems harassing the woman at home during wartime. Added responsibilities, worry over loved ones in the armed forces, shortage of household help, participation in civic activities—truly, legion are the demands. The task of carrying on efficiently is far more difficult than in peacetime.

It is absolutely vital that the housewife, the keystone of the home, should keep up her physical and mental energy. Only in that way can she wisely meet her myriad problems. Maintaining a stout front of courage and optimism is increasingly hard. But when one knows and practices the little secrets of recuperation, of "restoring oneself," the task is immeasurably lightened.

First, consider posture. A correct posture, one

in which the body is at ease, free from strain, is of the utmost importance in conserving and intelligently directing the energies. An unadjusted body, one that is out of alignment, tires easily. The unnatural strain on muscles and nerve-centers causes both mental and physical fatigue.

This cannot be completely remedied and the body properly aligned until, little by little, the muscular system is loosened and toned up and the breathing is so brought under control that it becomes natural and normal.

Turn to the exercises which were carefully designed for this very purpose—the *Three-way Breakdown,* explained in Chapter II, and the *Three-way Breath Control,* in Chapter III. Execute them repeatedly, step by step, and you will soon notice the difference in your carriage, the ease with which you can absorb strain, the all-round beneficial effect of proper posture and breathing.

Take the shoulders, for instance. To permit them to slump forward is to limit the breath capacity of the chest. To force them exaggeratedly back and attempt to hold them there is to build tension. But the easy rearward pull of the shoulders—Step *B* of the *Three-way Breath Control*—

Training aviation cadets, U.S. Army Air Forces, in relaxation. Capt. Paul P. George, Commanding Officer, looking on approvingly. Lester McDaniel, Assistant in "Miller Methods," at left.

Explaining "laws of flow" to Dad and Son, typical golfers.

brings about naturally an erect but relaxed position.

Recently a business man took the Miller Method for one reason only. His wife had criticized, pleasantly but vigorously, his habitually poor posture. Halfway through the course he drew me aside.

"I thought you were going to work with me on proper posture," he complained. "That is what I came for."

Without comment, I put him through the *Three-way Breakdown*. At the lowest point his body described a beautiful curve from the hips to the top of the head; and he came up easily and naturally by the three stages to an erect position.

"Now," I said, "bring your feet almost together, pointing directly forward....Right! Now walk into the next room and take a look at yourself in the mirror."

He faced the full-length mirror. With head set squarely, shoulders easily erect, breathing deeply and naturally, his image reflected perfect posture. A pleased grin stole across his face.

'What's wrong with that?" I asked.

"Why, it's all right!"

"It's excellent. Good posture comes naturally

when you loosen up the entire body gradually and then set it squarely back up the way it should be."

A second fundamental principle in lessening strain is that of letting the movable joints of the body take the flow of body-weight. They were designed for that exact and definite purpose. But do it easily, gracefully. Never "jam on the brakes" suddenly—any more than you would with a costly car.

Do you lean over a low table while working? Place the work on a higher plane or sit down to the task.

Every housewife stoops innumerable times, in picking up things, or in working in her prized Victory Garden. Do you bend *from the waist?* That induces strain at the base of the spine, often bringing on backache. Form the habit of lowering the body by bending the knees. Thus you let the leg and thigh muscles take the load.

The mother who picks up a baby many times should remember to bend her knees in stooping, and thus avoid undue strain.

There are authorities who advocate bending from the waist and keeping the knees straight, for the slimming effect on the waist. But why do a dangerous thing—"jam the knee-joints"—for the sake of weight reduction? Far better for this purpose are the *Handball Swing* and the *Cross-over Exercise*. Their twisting and bending movements will aid in melting surplus weight at the waist. At the same time, they will keep the knees flexible.

Handball Swing:

Stand with the feet comfortably apart (elbow-to-fingertip distance), hands on the hips, the knees bent, the breathing deep in the lower lungs.

Swing the left arm well rearward, twisting the hip.

Then sweep the arm down and up and forward again.

Return the left hand to the left hip.

At the lowest point of the downward swing the hand should almost brush the floor, and the left knee should be well bent.

Alternate, executing a long swing with the right arm.

Return the right hand to the right hip.

Do this exercise to the slow count of "1—2—3—4."

Cross-over Exercise:

Take the same position as in the *Handball Swing,* the hands on the hips.

Swing the right arm over the left leg and touch the floor with the fingertips of the right hand at the *farthest possible point* beyond the left foot.

As the fingertips of the right hand touch the floor, the left knee should be well bent. The right leg turns on the ball of the foot and the knee bends *almost to the floor.* This will bring the right foot up on the toe.

Return the right hand to the right hip.

Alternate the movement, swinging the left arm over the right leg and touching the floor at the farthest possible point beyond the right foot.

Execute each cross-over to the long count of "1—2—3—4."

Double-chin Exercise:

Hold the head well back and waggle the lower jaw up and down *widely.*

Turn the head to the right, with the chin held high, and repeat the waggling of the lower jaw.

To the center and repeat.

To the left, the chin high, and repeat.

Shake the head loosely to relieve any tension developed in this reducing exercise.

An excellent relaxing routine—if somehow you can manage the time from all your busy activities—is to take a short nap, or at least lie down and thoroughly relax, in the early or mid-afternoon. It need not be for long. Thirty minutes is ample. Then go through the exercises given in Chapters II and III. Follow with a quick hot bath; remaining too long in hot water has a weakening effect. End with a dash of cold water. It is invigorating. And it closes the pores and helps to ward off colds.

The time taken for this "siesta," followed by the muscle-toning and breath-control exercises, is not wasted. It restores one's strength to meet the demands of home-coming children and husband. Good health and spirits are contagious, radiating to all around one.

Let us consider now another major problem

of wartime—the women working in war industries. The woman at the lathe, the girl engaged in delicate operations involving intense concentration, the woman inspector who must be keenly alert, mentally and physically on tiptoe, as it were, the girl at a monotonous task over a bench, or even at a typewriter—all of them need full knowledge of the fundamental rules of relaxation, the art of "restoring oneself" as one works.

Sit squarely whenever you job permits. The crack musician in a leading band knows this secret of endurance. Only with his feet comfortably spread, shoulders squared but held naturally, his breath pumped from deep in the lower lungs, can he maintain a mellow tone in those long, difficult selections. Or there is the racing driver. He, too, sits squarely in his seat. He knows that only so can he withstand the incredible strains of his grueling profession.

Relax! Smooth-flowing movements pay dividends in increased output, regardless of the operation being performed. The rhythmic motion in the flying fingers of the winner in a touch-typing contest is evidence of this. Jerky movements definitely reduce over-all speed.

Try this simple test. Holding the arm and hand tense, make fast motions. Now take a long, deep breath and completely relax or loosen up the muscles. Suddenly flash the hand out. You will be convinced, as innumerable experiments have convinced the writer, that speed is increased from twenty-five to thirty per cent when the muscular system is free from tension.

We see this continually in sports. Apparently nonchalant, loosely hung ball players like Eddie Miller, of the Cincinnati Reds, and Marty Marion, of the St. Louis Cardinals, start like a flash. They can cover wide areas. "Flash" Gordon, Yankee star, in his movements the embodiment of ease, makes "hard plays look easy" in diamond parlance.

Then, too, smooth movements promote greater endurance. The chop-stroke tennis player, employing principally the forearm, is eventually worn down by an opponent using the full shoulder in stroking.

The woman worker engaged in either mental

or physical tasks should not discount the value of going through the relaxation exercises at the close of the day. They give one a complete physical check-over. They take out the "kinks" caused by too-long employment of one set of muscles. They stimulate the blood circulation, thus revitalizing all parts of the body. They loosen up and make more efficient the complex nervous system.

Try it for a week, going through the exercises once daily; preferably in the late afternoon at least an hour before eating. An indescribable sensation of well-being will reward you.

The three exercises in this chapter, the *Rhumba Movements* in Chapter IV, and exercise *B* of the *Body-flow Drills* in Chapter V, will give a balanced selection. They will improve flow and further induce over-all relaxation; and, with renewed buoyancy, you will find yourself taking those daily tasks and troubles "in stride."

CHAPTER IX

MILITARY RELAXATION

THERE IS NEED for complete relaxation in all
phases of military activity. A soldier on the march
can conserve his strength materially through correct body-flow by imitating the easy swing of the
woodsman. When he centers on a living target
over the sights of his gun he must be relaxed. If
he can remain loose while engaged in a bayonet
duel he has a distinct advantage over a tight-
muscled foe.

The officer on the bridge of his ship while
under fire; the naval gunner, on whose precise
operations depends the efficiency of his thunder-
ing charges; the radio operator; the signal man
and all others, benefit decidedly through the application of the principles of relaxation.

Perhaps above all, the man piloting an airplane

must master body-flow and relaxation. This should be begun with the primary training, the stage at which the aviation cadet actually first learns to fly. It is an exceedingly critical period. By far the greatest percentage of eliminations, or "wash-outs," take place here.

In considering physical education as applied to any field, the objective should be kept clearly in mind. For instance, in the sports world, the baseball player needs lighter training than the wrestler or the football player. The foot soldier slogging along under a heavy pack, obliged to surmount many obstacles, needs a great deal of body-building work, to increase his strength and endurance.

On the other hand, the flier, the major part of whose operations call for precise control and fluidity, requires special training in body balance, flow and relaxation. Mastery of these qualities leads, in turn, to the increased speed of his reflexes, invaluable to the flier in combat.

The youth going from civilian life into aviation is entering an almost completely foreign field. Some "carry-over" from familiar things in everyday life to basic principles of flying is quite helpful. He may recall the natural relaxation of the animals—the dog, the cat, the hare; or the way superior athletes demonstrate body-flow; even the looseness used by that neighborhood lad in expertly "tooling" his second-hand flivver around a corner. All of these demonstrate qualities needed by a good aviator.

One of the practical illustrations used by the writer, in working with United States Army aviation cadets, is that of the filled water glass. As

long as the movement of the hand is smooth or rhythmic no liquid will spill. But let the motion become jerky and the water will slop over. Similarly, the control-stick of a plane must be handled. Gradually-applied pressure is needed rather than strength.

Too much emphasis cannot be placed upon handling the stick in a relaxed manner. But we must go farther than that. The feet control the rudders. Therefore, it is essential that the lower half of the body be fluid. The hips, knees and ankles must be thoroughly loose. The simple

Rhumba Movements, given in Chapter IV, are ideally suited to this purpose.

The formula for incorporating in the body of the student flier the principles of complete body-flow and relaxation is practically identical with that employed for athletes.

First, the entire muscular structure is "un-locked" through the *Three-way Breakdown*—described in Chapter II. Second, cadets are taught deep and full breathing by the *Three-way Breath Control* exercises given in Chapter III. The *Body-flow Drills,* in Chapter V, conclude this phase.

The next step is to teach cat-like quickness. The *Five-step Balance Method,* outlined in Chapter V, largely achieves this end.

Finally, a series of progressive tests are given to ascertain the degree of complete relaxation, or "unit-flow," developed. Cadets are instructed at a signal to fall on their backs on the hardwood floor. Only by fine physical relaxation combined with the proper use of the joints can bruises be avoided. The *Dual Drill* and the *Spinning-top Test* (in Chapter V) provide further acid tests as to the student's mastery of body-flow. The *Spin-ning-top,* especially, calls for exceptional poise.

Fear, anger, tension, are evidenced by the same

general physical reactions—shortness of breath and a tightening of the muscular structure. Let the muscles go loose, lower the breath into the diaphragm, and you have gone far toward mastering these disturbances.

A reminder placed where it can be seen constantly helps. I suggested this to the aviation cadets. You can rely upon the ingenuity of the American youth. The next day I was proudly shown a strip of adhesive-tape pasted to the trouser-leg of a flying suit. On it, inked vertically, were the letters "R E L A X."

At the beginning of the course I explained to the assembled cadets that merely to go through the routines daily would help them only in a minor way. "You must make the principles of relaxation a part of your life," I insisted. "Pick a 'buddy.' Remind each other to remain relaxed at all times. If one of you sees the other tense at the study table, say, 'Relax.' If one is walking stiffly the other should remind him to 'loosen up.'"

Recalling my experiences and that of others, music was used in training. When stiffness or mechanical movements were present in learning flow routines, we sang the words of the *Blue*

Danube Waltz. A marked improvement in rhythm was noted.

Working thus, physically, mentally and psychologically, is it any wonder that fine results were achieved? There were more than a third less "wash-outs" or eliminations among those who took the Miller Method featuring body-flow and relaxation, as compared with those given only the orthodox training of calisthenics and acrobatics.

This is not meant in any way to depreciate the high value of acrobatics, calisthenics and similar body-building exercises. Youths coming from a comparatively "soft" civilian life into aviation unquestionably need a degree of "toughening up." They need the body-building exercises.

But for each minute spent in building power, at least another minute should go to teaching them to "unlock" that power, to make it flowing and therefore more efficient. The time spent during primary training in instilling complete relaxation is profitably expended.

An officer of the Army Air Forces, witnessing a demonstration of my Method as the cadets went through one of the fundamental exercises, asked a question.

"How do you think this training will affect a cadet mentally?"

"If we grant the premise that the human being is a unit," I replied, "that all sides of his nature—the physical, the nervous system and even the mind—are inextricably interlocked, isn't it logical to assume that when the physical structure is 'unlocked' step by step and the breathing properly adjusted, the mentality will benefit? I try to induce in the student the absolute consciousness of being relaxed."

CHAPTER X

BODY CONTROL IN SPORTS

MASTERY OF THE principles of body control enables a crack athlete to relax while under pressure. A football player coolly disregards onrushing opponents to whip a pass to a speeding teammate. A cager flashes down the basketball court. Suddenly going from intense action to repose he calmly shoots a goal. A baseball pitcher with three men on, the roar of an excited throng in his ears, throws a curve ball over the outside corner of the home plate. All know the value of remaining relaxed while in action.

The basic position for such sports as baseball, basketball, football, etc., is that used for most of the exercises in this book: The feet are stationed elbow-to-fingertip distance apart; as measured

Betty Rosenquest, a pupil of the author's, is now the nation's fourth ranking girl tennis star and the only junior to win the Women's Championship of New Jersey.

Glenn Dobbs, University of Tulsa, 1943 All-American half-
back, passing. One of the many football players taught
relaxation by the author.

from instep to instep, and the toes are pointed slightly outward.

From this position the athlete's perfect crouch is gained by letting the knees go *outward* squarely over the balls of the feet as the body is lowered. This outward movement of the knees is one of the basic laws of balance. Note the ballet dancer. Perfect balance is all-important in the difficult movements she must execute. She moves her knees outward instinctively.

During a stay in Los Angeles I had the opportunity to observe the close affinity between sports and dancing. Don Budge, Bobby Riggs, tennis aces, and the inimitable Francisco Seguro, South American star, in their agility and grace parallel Fred Astaire and Ray Bolger, top dancers, for instance. Both fields call for complete relaxation and body-flow.

The great athletes all work more fully into the knees than those less proficient. Bobby Jones, for

instance, in golf permits his rear knee to follow into the stroking movement more fully than per-

haps any golfer I have studied. Joe Platak, national handball champion, over six feet in height,
almost kneels on the floor in going after a low
ball. Bobby Riggs, tennis titleholder, makes practically impossible "gets" in tennis—principally
because he crouches exaggeratedly in the returning of low balls.

Some of my experiences in the sports world
may be of value to young athletes who are seeking to gain mastery in one or more fields through
perfect body control.

GOLF

One day I was working with a golfer friend.
We were trying to remove the "locks" from his
muscular system. Finally, I said smilingly, "Joe,
let's try something. Take your stance." He did so.

"Now laugh—as though you just heard a good
joke. Come on, open up! That's right. Now

swing that club back and hit the ball in a joyous, carefree manner. Forget technique. I don't care if you hit the ball ten feet or into those woods over there on the left."

I purposely turned my back and walked away —and turned again to see a white pellet soaring straight down the course into the blue. My friend's face was wreathed in a broad grin.

"Joe, I've been talking about easy power, the benefits of 'letting yourself go.' But have I said anything about accuracy?"

"No, Bill, you haven't."

"If you'd taken a ruler and laid out its course that ball couldn't have sailed a truer flight. Remember, when you completely follow-through you get not only added power but deadly accuracy as well."

The technique of a given sport—how to hold a golf club, tennis racket, baseball or football—is of relatively minor importance. Good body control, plus relaxation, spells the difference between the champion and the average performer.

A golf professional will instruct his pupil to follow-through on his swing. It is pre-eminently sound advice. But only through complete body flow can this be done.

The pupil commences his swing, but when a certain point is reached the club head pulls off the line of flow. Why? Probably because the shoulders are stiff or "locked." Let us suppose, however, that the shoulders are quite loose. The club head swings accurately in a longer curve. But just before the end of the swing it veers off once more. Glancing down, you will probably notice that the knee is stiff, thus preventing the rear leg from following the body movement.

Only by completely loosening up the muscles leading into all the joints—the shoulders, hips, knees, ankles—can one follow-through to the ultimate point.

TENNIS

Several years ago I sat in a West Coast stadium. Out on the white-lined tennis court two of the

leading racket wielders of the nation fought fiercely. They were seemingly well matched in ground strokes, in net work, in strategy of play, etc. But one was gradually gaining ascendancy over the other. Yet only in service was he superior.

Frequently, the man who was winning smashed unreturnable first balls across the net. His opponent's service lacked viciousness. Wherein lay the difference? Physically, they seemed on a par, both being tall and of rangy build. Both used the same type of service, the popular "American twist." But there the similarity ended.

One simply hit the ball with an arm and shoulder movement. His stance at the finish of the serve was with the left foot still in advance of the right. But the other man attained maximum power. Using the ball of the left foot as a pivot-point, his right leg came completely over. Then the full power of the big back and shoulder muscles, plus the right side, was smashed into the finish. At the close of the service the right foot was advanced beyond the left.

BOWLING

Ned Day, world's match bowling champion, in action is a study in effortless ease. Coolly, calmly, he positions the ball in both hands. Every muscle is relaxed. His breath is deep in the diaphragm. Then smoothly, he goes into his fluid delivery. As he steps forward he drops naturally into a lower plane. His forward glide is like that of a panther on a carpet of leaves. And when the ball leaves his hands at the finish of the delivery there is a barely audible whisper of sound as the ball meets the hardwood.

Day's balance, co-ordination and control are superb. Let the camera catch him just as the ball leaves his hand and it will find him in perfect balance. The left arm is extended and the right leg is well over to the left and to the rear of the left leg, compensating for the weight of the ball. The front knee is well bent, taking the flow of weight without strain.

HANDBALL

I had the pleasure of co-operating with Joe Platak, eight times national handball king, in the School of Skills at the Tulsa Y.M.C.A. Matchless Joe had just finished a week of instruction in his sport. I had studied him closely every day. The big Hungarian was indeed an absorbing subject.

Platak's stance while awaiting a return reminded one of an old Negro mammy at the wash-
tub. He was as loose as a wet dishrag, utterly relaxed. His arms hung at his sides. The knees
were slumped. But then came a ball in the back
court. Smoothly Joe slid into position. His arm
and shoulders flowed into the stroke—and suddenly, incredibly, there was an explosion of
smashing power. The ball caromed off the end
wall, virtually unreturnable.

I came to certain conclusions. One day I tackled
Platak. "Joe, how about being a guinea-pig?"

Big Joe grinned amiably. "It's O.K. by me.
What's on your mind?"

"I'd like to analyze you for our final audience.
And I'd rather not tell you what I'm going to
say. You can reply if you wish. Throw rocks if
you want to."

To the assemblage I stated: "Folks, we have
had with us one of the greatest handball players
of all time, a super-athlete. All week he has been
showing us the proper method of hitting a ball,
the devices by which he deceives his opponent,
and so forth. But now I'm going to try and show
you the real secrets of his greatness."

I pointed out Platak's calm attitude. Grasping

his biceps in both hands I shoved his big shoulder upward. So loose was it that it almost touched his ear. I drew attention to his deep breathing— from the "bellows." I concluded: "You've all seen Joe go after a low ball. Practically kneeling on the court. This knee is as flexible as his elbow."

Platak was kind enough to state that I had pointed out things of which he himself had not been fully aware.

VOLLEY BALL

Web Caldwell, acting physical director of the Los Angeles Y.M.C.A., was a former all-round athlete. He had won All-American recognition at volley ball. Through mutual experimentation we found that several cardinal principles of body balance held good in this sport.

Ahead of the play the crouched position described at the beginning of this chapter should be assumed. Thus, with the weight on the balls of the feet, the knees well bent, the player is prepared to move instantaneously in any direction.

The hands should be turned palms upward. Especially is this true when stationed in the rear line. A hard serve which clears the front trio usually comes in low. By maintaining a crouched position with hands held palms upward, an effective return can be made.

There is an excellent drill which greatly improves quick-starting ability:

The players are formed in a circle. Each is given a number. All assume a crouched position. The ball is tossed into the exact center of the ring as a player's number is called. He should reach the sphere before it falls to the floor and bat it to the "feeder." As players become more proficient, the circumference of the circle is increased.

This drill improves the ability of the players to get the ball to the "spiker." Also it throws the spotlight on the unready player.

BADMINTON

Badminton is a game in which the average player may be inclined to disregard the fundamental rules for balance and quick-starting. There are several logical reasons for this. First, the playing space is rather limited, especially when playing doubles. The need is not fully recognized for instantaneous speed. Second, shots are executed with a flexed wrist or a "whipping" motion, in direct contrast to the "locked" wrist used in tennis.

But when a professional badminton champion visited our city he gave a striking demonstration of the value of balance and complete muscular flow. His body was a revelation in the art of utilizing every ounce of power. Especially was this noticeable in making a "kill." His back arched. Then like a sprung bow it whipped into the smash.

Following this exhibition, his young son took the court against a local boy. Now, the professional's son was much better versed in the technique and strategy of play than the other. Yet, to the amazement of all, the local boy won. It so happened that the lad was an all-round athlete. He had also taken a course in body control. This again proved the truth of the theory I have already stated. In the human body rather than in technical knowledge lies the answer to excelling in sports.

FOOTBALL

Glenn Dobbs, All-American back of Tulsa University, was naturally gifted. Tall and with

a long arm he whipped a football around with
exceptional skill. But fundamentally two structural weaknesses held him back from true greatness. First, he ran a little stiff-legged. Second, his
shoulder movement ended too soon. The first
handicapped him in dodging while running.
Both lessened his power and accuracy in passing
the ball to a distant player.

How were these things corrected? This hard-
working, conscientious player spent a long time
practicing phase *C* of the *Three-way Breakdown*
(explained in Chapter II). The muscles leading
into his knees were thus freed from tension.

Then the upper back and shoulder muscles
were loosened up thoroughly. This permitted the
shoulder used in passing to follow-through completely, ending its movement flush against the
chin. Thus maximum power and accuracy were
gained.

Previously Dobbs had been extremely accurate
in passing into "the flat" or to medium distance.
But when the range was extended that stiff knee

had cut off the complete flow of body-weight—
just as the golfer's swing is retarded by this factor. When the knee was able to bend freely forward,
ward, maximum power was achieved.

Practically all sport fans are familiar with the
outstanding achievement of the tall Oklahoman
in the Sugar Bowl Game at New Orleans on New
Year's Day, 1943. Against the powerful Tennes-
see team he rifled seven consecutive passes (six to
the same great receiver, Sax Judd) for a touchdown.

Also they know his work in the 1943 College
All-Star-Professional game at Chicago. In this
contest he out-passed the illustrious Sammy Baugh,
Washington Redskin "ace," both in percentage
of completions and in number of yards per com-
pletion. Dobbs completed *nine passes in thirteen
attempts.*

But some of his other sensational records are
not as commonly known. For instance, during
the 1942 season with Tulsa University he completed 67 of 107 attempted passes, for a comple-
tion percentage of .626, *leading the nation* in this
respect. During the 1943 season he was again
chosen All-American with the nation's All-
Service team. He tied with Sid Luckman, of the

Chicago Bears, in *setting a world's record of seven touchdown passes* in one game for the Randolf Air Base team.

Basketball

Basketball, with its lightning-like changes of play and its sudden starts and stops, demands exceptional balance and flow. Nat Holman, of the New York Celtics, Forest "Red" DeBernardi, of the Kansas City Cooks, "Jumping Jack" Mc-Cracken, of Denver American Legion, Bart Carlton, of the Tulsa Oilers, and "Hank" Luisetti, Stanford star, were the clearest evidence of the value of complete relaxation in this fast game. All were magnificent performers.

Take Luisetti, for example. He does not necessarily rank above the others I have named, but he has more recently than any of the others played from coast to coast. Many thousands of players have tried to master his famed one-hand shot, and few have succeeded.

They hold the ball as Luisetti does—on a flat plane just above the right eye. They station the right foot directly under the right hand, the shooting hand. They push the ball upward in earnest imitation of his shots. But the real secret of Luisetti's uncanny accuracy lies in that long loose body. His arm is supple. Shoulder and back and hip and knee and ankle are flexible. Luisetti has complete body-flow. There is nothing to pull the shooting hand off its horizontal plane, level with that of the goal rim.

Luisetti also has cat-like reactions, as have all really expert players. From whence does this muscular quickness stem? Did you ever watch a cat, a mouse, or a hare? Soft as velvet, pliable as silk, at a sudden sound they are gone. Emulate these athletes and animals. Relax!

BASEBALL

While living in Pennsylvania as a boy, my father took me to Pittsburgh's Forbes Field. There I saw the great Honus Wagner play. The famed "Flying Dutchman" covered the area around shortstop like a tent, to use a trite expression. As steel to a magnet, so the ball seemed to attract itself to those great paws.

I have since tried to analyze his uncanny fielding ability. One thing I distinctly recall. His big glove, stationed at the right foot, was always completely open to the oncoming ball. Mediocre players often half close the glove.

An important last reminder to players just before entering a game may well be: *"Open your hands ahead of the play!"*

The extent of glove-surface presented to the ball is important. But to a great fielder like Wagner other parts of the body were as important as the hand itself in pulling down a ball. When Wagner's glove met the ball squarely his great loose frame seemed literally to turn inside out. His left hip and knee swung widely inward to permit the full turn of the left shoulder and arm. His flow and flexibility stemmed basically from his genial nature. He was always relaxed, both mentally and physically.

How can the poorer performer attain the same objective? By loosening up the muscles of the entire body. Then and then only can the body "follow the glove."

Again, let us consider the art of throwing. The poor player, I find, usually straightens up after fielding a ball. The throw is made with the arm only. Accurate throwers remain crouched at a three-quarter level until the entire movement is completed. The body seems to "lie out" in the air. The knees stay bent, taking the flow of weight without a hitch. They thus avoid "throwing the brakes" too suddenly.

CHAPTER XI

RELAXATION IN DAILY LIFE

MANY ATTEMPT TO CROWD a full week's exercise into a day or two days over the week-end. They rush frenziedly into physical activities of all kinds —hiking, swimming, golf, tennis. The inevitable result is harm to the system rather than good. Muscular soreness and fatigue are the aftermath.

No week-ender can drive himself without let-up all day and then, on going home, expect to find complete relaxation. The woodsman's secret, the secret of the top athlete, and of the animals, is that of recuperation, of "restoring oneself" as one works. In other words, the art of relaxing under pressure.

The routines given in this book—"unlocking" the muscular system, breath control, and the other exercises—are definitely helpful in bringing about complete circulation and flow to the system. They have been given simply and clearly so they may be easily mastered. But no matter how simple the routines, it is apparent that few individuals will follow them with complete regularity.

In checking at a considerably later date those who have taken my relaxation course, two things have been noted. First, they have at times lapsed from faithfully practicing the routines daily. But when they found themselves becoming strained or tense, they knew the remedy. Several days' resumption of the routine invariably straightened out their condition.

Second, and more important, they know how to apply the principles of relaxation to daily living. Relaxation can be made a "part of one." It is the way you take that first step in walking, the manner in which you first sit down at that desk each morning, the way in which you climb into bed at night, that count. Let us analyze some of these things.

WALKING

Before taking that first step, glance down at your feet. Are they positioned correctly, pointing

straight forward? Are they spaced comfortably—
approximately the width of four fingers apart?

Now press the "magic button." With the arms
full-length at the sides, slowly raise the muscles
of the upper half of the body. Simultaneously
slowly draw the breath up into the chest. Then
let the muscles down ("let go" clear to the toes)
and lower the breath into the diaphragm. This
deep, gentle adjustment of the system makes for
complete relaxation.

Step out with a comfortably long stride; not
exaggerated, but of sufficient length to demand
good movement of the hips. As you walk, breathe
deeply from the lower lungs. Avoid jerky strides.
Mentally visualize yourself as "flowing along,"
not simply walking.

If you find yourself hurrying unduly, as even
the best of us do at times, pause an instant to
check yourself. Make the muscle-and-breath adjustment again, then resume your way. You will
find that a smooth way of moving will "eat up
the ground" just as quickly as taking long strides,
and you will be building relaxation.

One well might imitate the Southern Negro's
way of walking. Note how loosely he swings
along, shoulders, hips, knees—in fact, the en-

tire body—flowing in unconscious but perfect rhythm.

Correct walking involves the continual flexing of the knees. Among its many advantages, it considerably lessens one's chances of injury in traffic. An illustration is an incident that happened to me. To my left as I stepped off a curb was a Stop sign. Approaching it fast was an automobile. The car, for some reason, did not pause at the warning sign. Instantaneously I sprang backward—onto the curb.

I had had no thought of impending danger. But my front foot had taken a customary long stride. The knees were well flexed and the weight on the balls of the feet. This structural balance made possible a sudden involuntary move out of danger. On the other hand, a short step and stiff knees probably would have made instantaneous movement impossible.

SITTING AT A DESK

Start the day's work right. Sit down at that desk in a relaxed manner, breathing deeply from the diaphragm. Stay that way. Let all movements be smooth and rhythmic, rather than jerky. For instance, in the act of writing let the arm work from the shoulder. Avoid tension.

Every office worker—and all others taking my course—is given a card on which is typed:

RELAX!

1. *Loosen Up!* All over.
2. *Adjust Body!* Muscle and Breath-control Method.

This reminder is placed in the top drawer of the desk, or under a plate-glass top, or in any place where it will immediately catch the eye. It reminds one to take the following steps:

Loosen Up: Placing the feet comfortably apart, relax all the joints—arms, shoulders, hips, knees, ankles—gently. Loosen up *all over.*

Adjust Body: Use the same simple adjustment as before the initial step in walking—explained earlier in this chapter.

There are several little practical habits which aid in maintaining relaxation, or restoring oneself, as one works. When engaged in conversation with another, sit in a calm relaxed way. Keep the fingers of the hand, wherever placed, comfortably open. Clenching the hand creates tension, which is transmitted clear up to the top of the spine.

Break up concentrated desk work by standing occasionally while answering the telephone. Stand loosely, breathing deeply from the lower lungs while you carry on the conversation.

Even in a brief visit to the water-cooler, you can relieve tension. Revolve the shoulders, loosen up, let yourself go slack.

An advertising executive, a member of one of the groups taking the Miller Method, told me that when at a complete loss for ideas he puts on his hat and goes for a brief stroll. He said that he was able to think more constructively on returning to his desk.

He had learned the beneficial effect of complete physical relaxation, and the resultant mental relaxation which brought renewed vigor to the mind.

SLEEPING

Sound sleep invariably follows complete relaxation. But just how can our systems be put in this desirable condition? The following are some ideas which have proved helpful to many.

Standing alongside the bed, loosen up the entire structure. Let the body go slack; relax gently all joints. Then simply raise one leg to the bed and follow with the other. Lie flat on the back, the feet comfortably apart and the arms fulllength at the sides. Open and relax the fingers.

This is simply a suggested starting position. There is no one correct position in which to sleep. The important thing is to remain "loose".

Next, check the breathing to make sure that it is coming deeply from the lower lungs. Raise the arms slowly until they are in a vertical position, simultaneously drawing the breath up into the chest. Let the arms drop slowly, letting the breath out through slightly parted lips and down once more into the diaphragm. As the arms near the surface of the bed, let them fall limply. Let yourself go completely, clear to the toes.

If complete structural looseness fails to induce sleep, try the mental relaxing method.

Starting with the scalp, concentrate, step by step, on your body down to your feet. Think deliberately about utterly relaxing each part. Successively, think of the top of the head as being loose and relaxed; the eyes being "heavy as lead"; the lower jaw falling; the shoulders, the arms, the hips, the knees, the ankles, each being relaxed in turn.

There is a very common cause of the inability to sleep well. This is the "squirrel-cage" of thoughts. Round and round they go. Business problems, personal worries, the next day's tasks, clutter up the mind until the poor victim tosses, wide-awake, for seemingly endless hours.

Deliberately transferring the mind to thoughts of things which convey peace and calm has been found very helpful. This, of course, would vary with the individual. With some it may be a garden of fragrant flowers, with bees and butterflies hovering about; the rhythmic drone of the bees, the graceful drifting of the butterflies, the remembered fragrance of sun-warmed blossoms, are soothing and peaceful.

With others there is nothing more sleep-provoking than the thought of a field of grain shimmering beneath the sun's rays; or a quiet pool in the woods, not a ripple disturbing its calm surface.

With yet others it might be thoughts of fishing. "It's so hot. I'm so lazy and tired. Too tired to even fish. Think I'll take a nap." So might run the thoughts. The head falls over to one side—sleep steals over one.

One of these methods—or a combination of the physical, mental and psychological patterns—is almost guaranteed to bring about the blessed boon of sound slumber.

CPSIA information can be obtained
at www.ICGtesting.com
Printed in the USA
BVHW041643081221
623539BV00010B/806